Black&White

Geometric Abstractions of
Edwin Mieczkowski

Presented by:
The Cleveland Artists Foundation
May 18 - July 28, 2012

Curated by:
Christopher L. Richards
MA Art History Candidate,
Kent State University

Edwin Mieczkowski
Born 1929, Pittsburgh PA.
MFA, Carnegie Mellon University, Pittsburgh, PA.
BFA, Cleveland Institute of Art, Cleveland OH.
1966 Cleveland Arts Prize

Lenders to the exhibition:
Rachel Davis Fine Arts
Constance Erdelac
LewAllen Contemporary
D. Wigmore Fine Art
Private Collection
Progressive Art Collection
Tregoning and Co.
Dave Tully

Staff Support:
Lauren Hansgen, Executive Director
Christine Radomski, Assistant to the Director

Published by Cleveland Artists Foundation, Cleveland, OH

Introduction by Lauren Hansgen
Essay by Christopher L. Richards
Edited by Christine Radomski

Design: Christopher L. Richards
Photo Credit: Christopher L. Richards, unless otherwise noted.
        Coutesy of D. Wigmore Fine Art: *Small Block, Warsaw #1,*
                Munchin' Henries at Shaky Heights
        Coutesy of LewAllen Contemporary: *Ice Rack, Prominera*
        Courtesy of Tregoning and Co.: *Furnace II, Galactica, Logic Loc*

INTRODUCTION

Lauren Hansgen
Executive Director
Cleveland Artists Foundation

Cleveland Artists Foundation is honored to present a selection of work by one of our region's greatest artistic treasures. Edwin Mieczkowski's contributions pervade countless discussions of Cleveland's artistic legacy—his reputation not just as artist, but as teacher and inspiration to those who have worked in the decades after he first made his mark here. The impact of geometric abstraction is powerful in its timelessness; these compositions are as visually arresting today as they were at their inception.

As always, Cleveland Artists Foundation is indebted to many individuals whose hard work, time, patience, and generosity have made this exhibition and catalog possible. My sincerest thanks goes to the lenders to the exhibition, Christine Radomski and each of our loyal volunteers, and the CAF Board of Directors, specifically the Programming Committee and Joan Brickley and Bill Tregoning who offered insights and resources early in the creation of this exhibition. I'd also like to thank Lawrence Sisson, who in being so generous with his time, performed conservation work on a piece from the CAF collection in spite of a very tight timeline, allowing us to display the work in this exhibition. We are proud and honored to present the curatorial work of Christopher L. Richards, who in producing this exhibition has also taken steps towards the completion of his MA in Art History at Kent State University. Christopher has been with CAF for a number of years, first as a volunteer and then as an intern, and has approached numerous projects — research, collections management, and myriad other tasks — with dedication and enthusiasm.

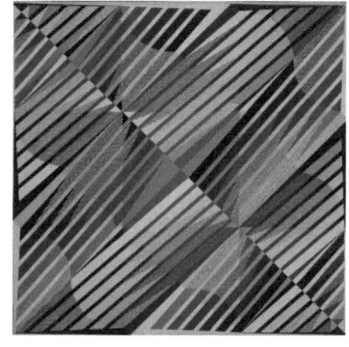

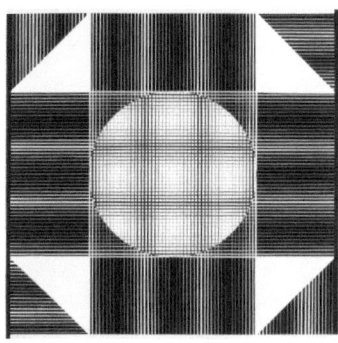

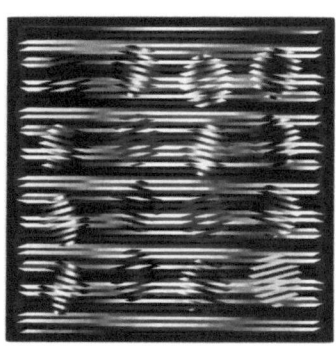

BLACK & WHITE: Edwin Mieczkowski   Christopher L. Richards

Looking at art created in black and white can open new vistas for viewers to re-examine how the world around them is perceived. The work of Edwin Mieczkowski is often celebrated for its use of bold color, with the work in black and white relegated to discussions of his 1960s Anonima Group activities. However, Mieczkowski used black and white in a striking and equally bold manner throughout his career with concepts based on science and perceptual psychology, building upon theories of non-objective art movements that came before him. Working in the two, and their tonalities, allowed this body of work to push the boundaries of geometric abstraction within its limited palette. Even' when used in his colored works, black and white holds a key role to how Mieczkowski's pieces are read and understood by the viewer.

Deliberate thought on working in black and white in terms of method was perhaps first realized for Mieczkowski while teaching a course on stone lithography at Carnegie Tech in 1957. Having had no experience in the medium, he set out to learn as his students did in a collaborative atmosphere. One of his students by the name of Francis Hewitt would become an important contributor. The two discussed the relationship between the preparatory drawings and the actual print making process, concluding that they preferred the former. Hewitt completed his degree and went on to study at Oberlin University for his masters, and Mieczkowski was offered a position at the Cleveland Institute of Art. Shortly after, Hewitt also joined the faculty at the Institute, where he

Top to Bottom:
Topopatop, 1965
Acrylic on masonite
24 x 24 inches
Private Collection

Ernst Benkert
Warsaw #1, 1964
Acrylic on masonite
24 x 24 inches
D. Wigmore Fine Art

Francis Hewitt
Munchin' Henries at Shaky Heights,
1965. Acrylic on masonite
24 x 24 inches
D. Wigmore Fine Art

and Mieczkowski continued their exploration in drawing by developing a course on Dimensional Drawing.

The goal of the course was to express space on a two-dimensional surface through pen and ink drawings. "We were passionate in our belief that size differences, overlap events, and brightness differences were critical to such a language and took precedence over systematic perspective,"[1] wrote Mieczkowski. After Hewitt introduced Mieczkowski to Ernst Benkert, the three artists began to share ideas and concepts, as well as a distaste for Abstract Expressionism. The ideas developed for the drawing course at the Cleveland Institute of Art would become the foundation upon which the Anonima Group would be formed.

Reacting against the existential drama of Abstract Expressionism, the Anonima Group began working together in 1960 and asserted that the art world was embracing sensationalism without the use of the intellect. Mieczkowski wrote, "Our time is now complicated by the too uncritical acceptance of the view that art is an emotive language, that it is arrived at through emotional frenzy. Feeling, mood and sentiment prevail and thought is downgraded as merely hindrance."[2] Issues were also brought up with Op artists who worked within the Gestalt psychological theories of perception – where the human eye sees objects as a whole before seeing the indivuidual parts – which the three artists felt were being over explored.[3] While they employed Gestalt theories themselves, the Anonima Group further developed their work by researching and investigating American experimental psychology,[4] in particular, the writings of James J. Gibson. His work focused on two-dimensional treatments of the visual world, and the Anonima Group desired to explore depth perception on a flat surface without the use of perspective. They also drew distinctions between art and science. Affirming that they were not scientists themselves, Mieczkowski commented in "Painting and Prediction:"

> Painting does not stress predictability as does science. Science, in establishing predictability, strives to give us the assurance of a constant world. Painting may

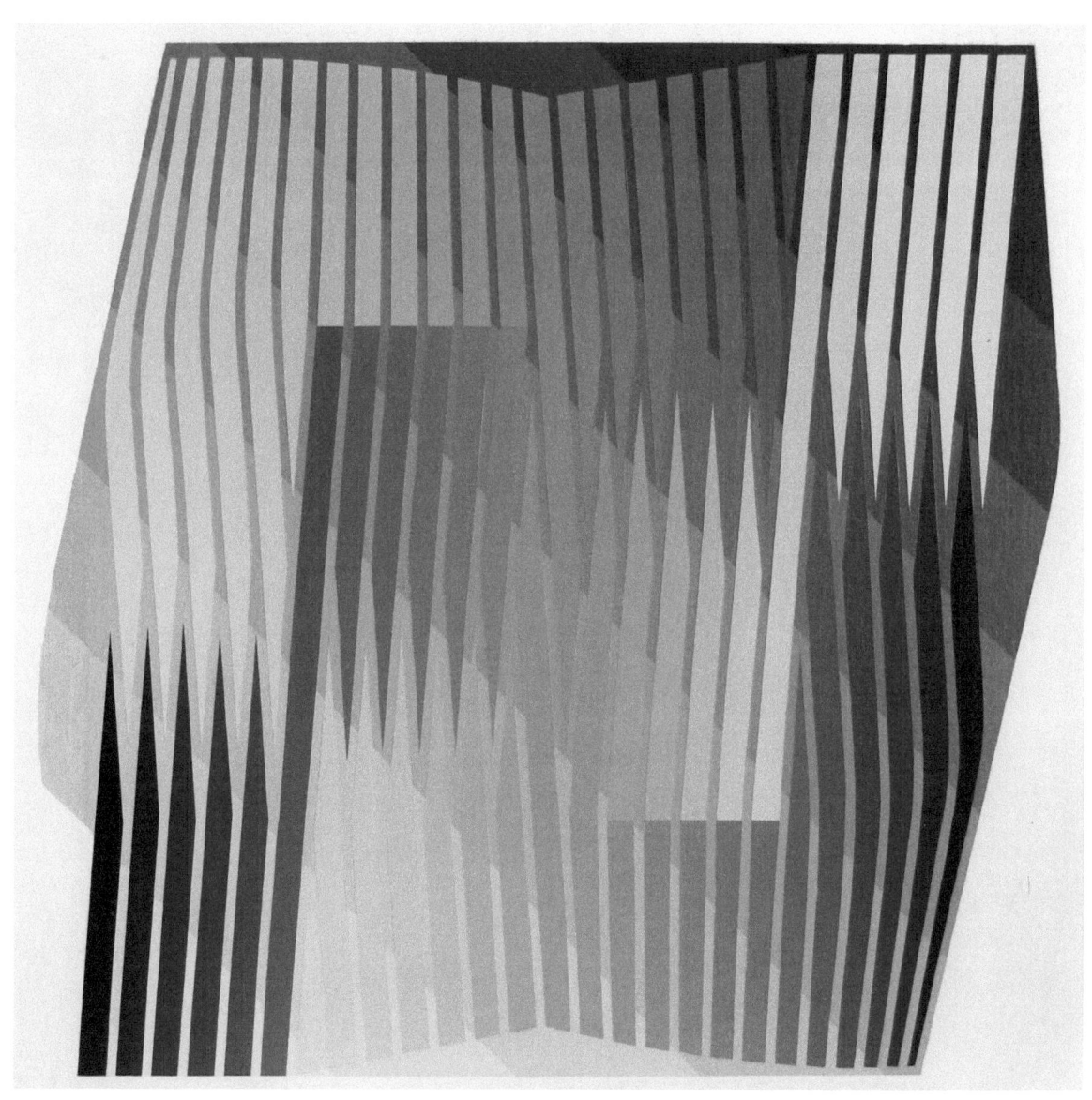

Study for ISO-Rung, 1965
Acrylic on masonite
30 x 30 inches
Rachel Davis Fine Arts

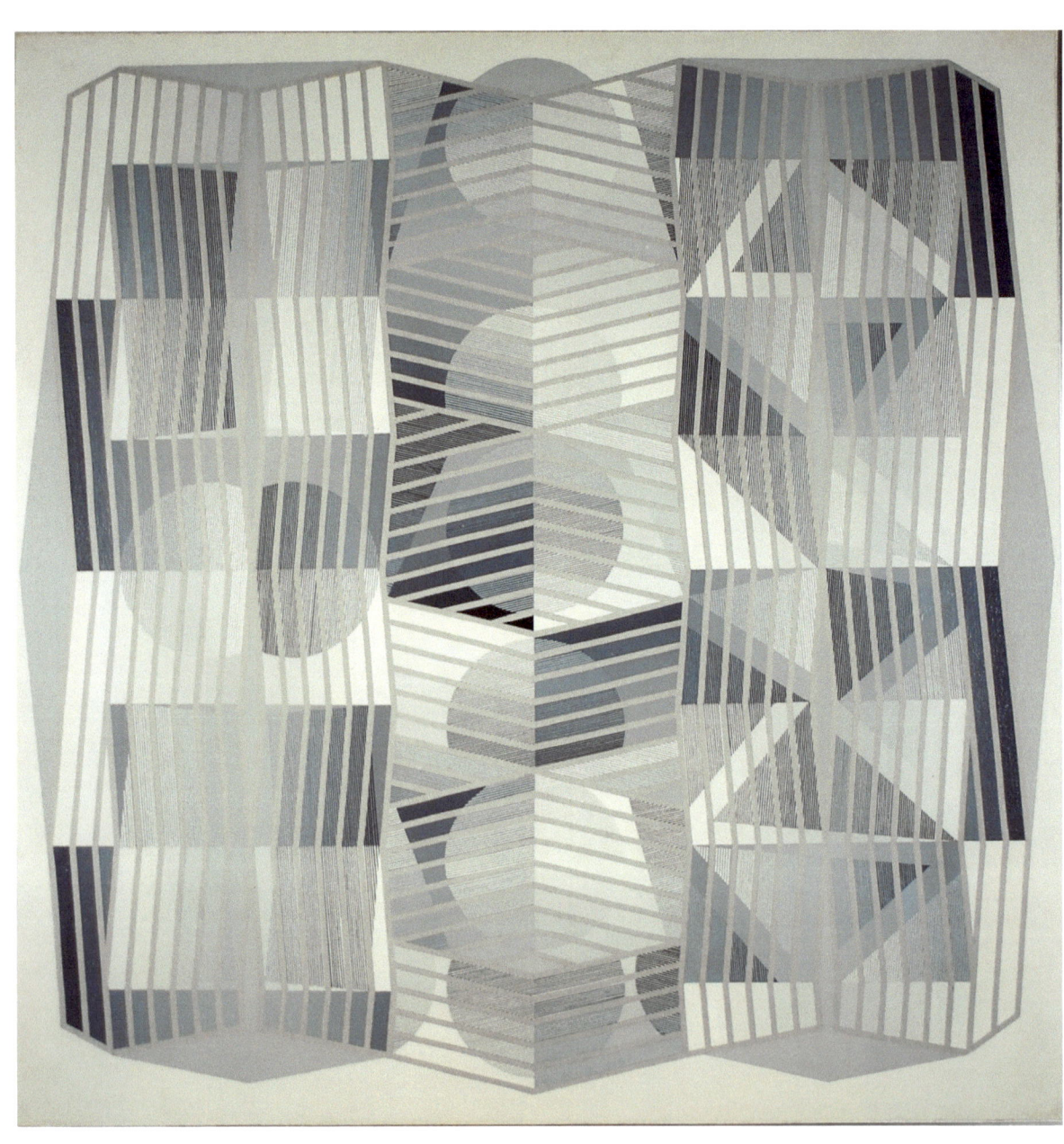

Untitled, ISO-Metric series, 1965
Acrylic on masonite
44 x 41.5 inches
Cleveland Artists Foundation Collection
Collector's Circle Purchase

use some of science's findings and set them up with apparent machine-like logic, but man-as-artist usurps their absoluteness when he manipulates them in structures of his own.[5]

The Anonima Group exploited black and white compositions for several purposes. First, this scheme allowed for a restriction of personal expression often made through the choice of color. It created a sense of anonymity, allowing the paintings to become that of the group over that of the individual. Exhibitions of their work were often hung together and pieces were left unsigned, or signed on the back, pushing the intellectual concepts to the forefront. Secondly, by limiting the palette to black, white, and grey, each artist was more capable of exploring the basic visual stimuli they had been researching in a way in which it would also be more easily understood by the viewer. Color, though not completely abandoned, was not necessary to examine principles of perceptual psychology, a branch of cognitive psychology pioneered by Gibson that focused on the mental processes used in everyday living. It was also unneeded to explore the concepts proposed by the Anonima Group's four year plan of finding solutions to overlap, relative size change, brightness ratio, and light and shade.

In the untitled 1965 painting from the *ISO-Metric series*, the mathematical use of the grids is set up to initially reassure the viewer by giving a sense of familiarity throughout the composition.[6] Mieczkowski also used the grid to raise mental strain and visual stress in the viewer by denying the comfort found in redundancy. He achieves this by vertically bisecting the painting into two halves, and at the same time dividing it into thirds that would predictably be viewed in the Gestalt Law of Similarity where similar shapes – like the circles in the center column – are seen as being grouped together.

The use of overlap in the grid disrupts a perceived predictability and fractures the picture plane, requiring the painting to be viewed and examined in sections rather than taken in as a whole. Viewers may become frustrated, but it is an attempt to force a slight increase in perception which the Anonima Group felt could affect a change in world sensibilities. Francis Hewitt hoped that paintings like this would be "elevating in the way that Mondrian used to talk about the New Society. It would make people really look at art, and it would lift you to heights of perception you never really understood before."[7]

By bisecting the composition, Mieczkowski initially allows the viewer to assume that the image is mirrored. The center column divided down the middle sets a program of opposite values, one side the ground begins as white while the other begins as black. This theme does persist throughout the painting, but his use of shape breaks the mirrored effect that central-ized viewing predicts. The left side relies on a polygon, circle, polygon pattern. The right side becomes increasingly confusing with the use of thick lines converging at sharp angles that do not repeat, even though a quick glance would lead the viewer to believe they do. Instead, the angles shift slightly as they near the bottom of the painting. Depending upon individual viewer perception, the angles can accomplish several actions. They become obscured by the line dividing light and dark or they can be seen to connect to the lower, mirrored angle forming a single line that horizontally shifts from light to dark. Circles in the painting are cut off though the eye wants to see them in entirety. This falls back on Gestalt theories, but is also part of the overlap plan that forces the circles into the background, laying behind the plane that disrupts them.

From the *Overlap series*, *Small Block* utilizes a quarter circle shape – a motif Mieczkowski would return to in the 2000s with a more painter-ly quality – that creates a circle and square overlap pattern. The black, white, and grey shapes lay one on top of another to form a push and pull of perceptual space. Mieczkowski used both high and low contrast sections in two different grid systems to create a further sense of depth and clarity. The centrally divided grid contains a stark black and white overlap that distinguishes crisp edges, while the secondary grid

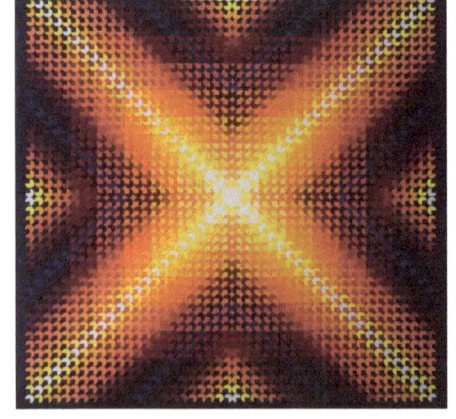

Furnace II, 2007
Acrylic on canvas
36 x 36 inches
Tregoning and Co.

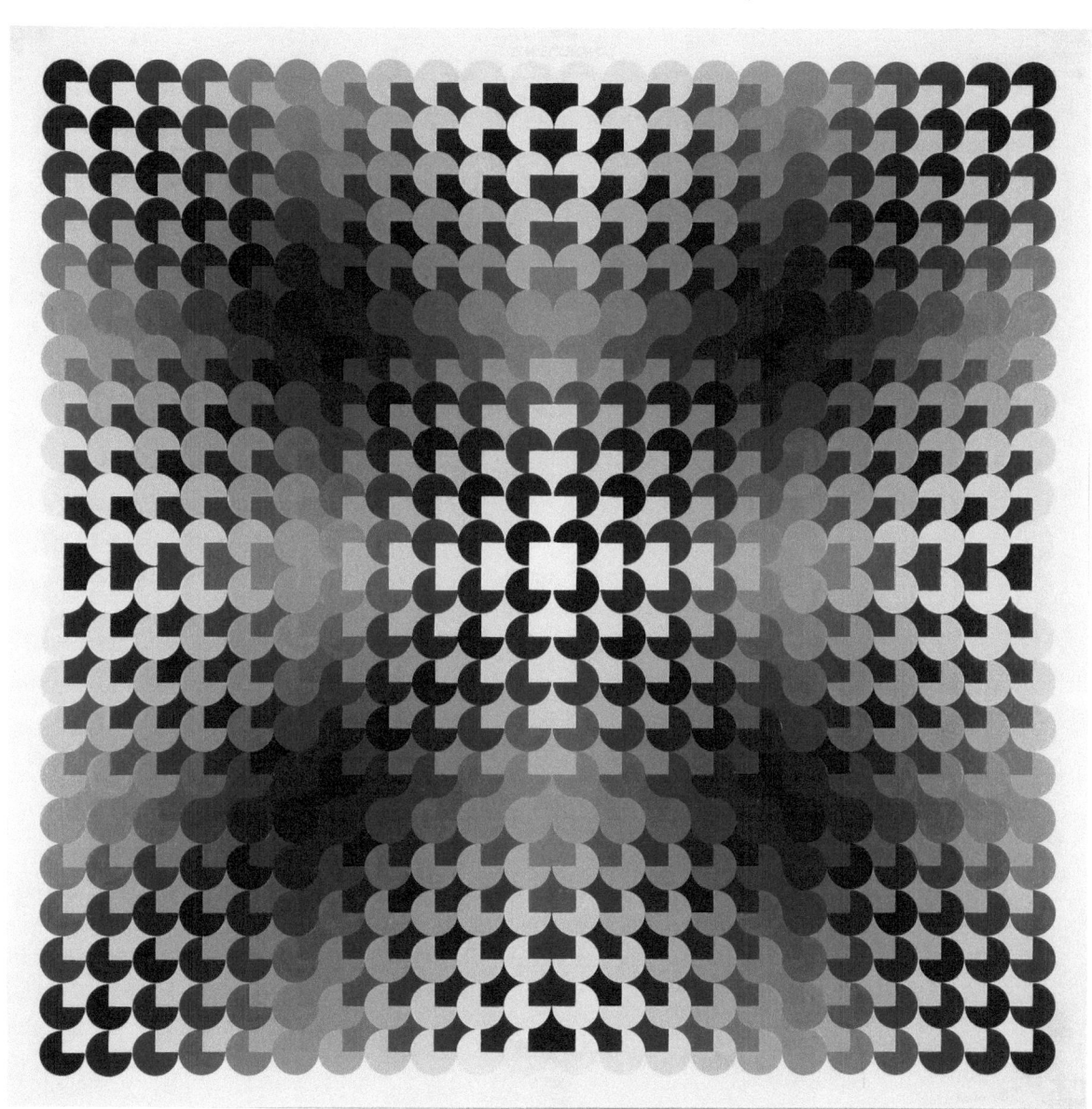

Small Bloc #2, 1966
Acrylic on masonite
24 x 24 inches
D. Wigmore Fine Art

system that cuts the composition into thirds contains shapes that range from light to dark grey in a gradient. The result is a central point in sharp focus that appears on the surface of the painting, while the gradient creates a soft blurring effect as if it recedes back into space.

Though it may initially speed up the viewers glances, the complexity of simple overlapping shapes and back and forth from light to dark in both of these Anonima period paintings ultimately forces the viewer to slow down in order to understand the process and purpose of the painting. This creates a motivational activity in line with the Transactional Theory of Perception. The viewer, rather than simply being a passive collector of visual information, must actively gather cues about the work. The participation of the viewer with the painting is the ultimate goal of the Anonima Group for it creates a change in the viewer's idea of the work that is not merely optical.

These rigid modes of creation continued to influence Mieczkowski's work after the Anonima Group dissolved in 1971. The group had disbanded prior to completing their four year plan, leaving light and shade an unexplored program. Mieczkowski's work in the 1970s reflects those concepts with works like *Ice Rack*. Its relationship to his work in brightness ratio is evident in the grid system and use of solid black, white, or grey rectangles. The arrangement of the darker greys and blacks lifts them to the foreground, while the low contrast of the whites and light greys recede.

The observations that are made with this painting are based on the organization of the rectangles. Grouped together, the darker rectangles overpower the lighter, allowing them to be perceived as creating a larger shape. The lighter portion of the piece creates two similar shapes on the left and right sides of the composition. This could inflict figure/ground reversals, however, the centrality of the darker shapes gives them visual priority over the other groupings. Adding to the dominance of the central dark area is the elongated horizontal shapes of the rectangles. Being surrounded by two groupings of lighter rectangles, a sense of landscape is created where the two opposite

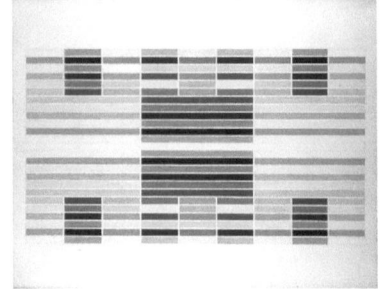

Ice Rack, c. 1978
Acrylic on paper
22 x 30 inches
LewAllen Contemporary

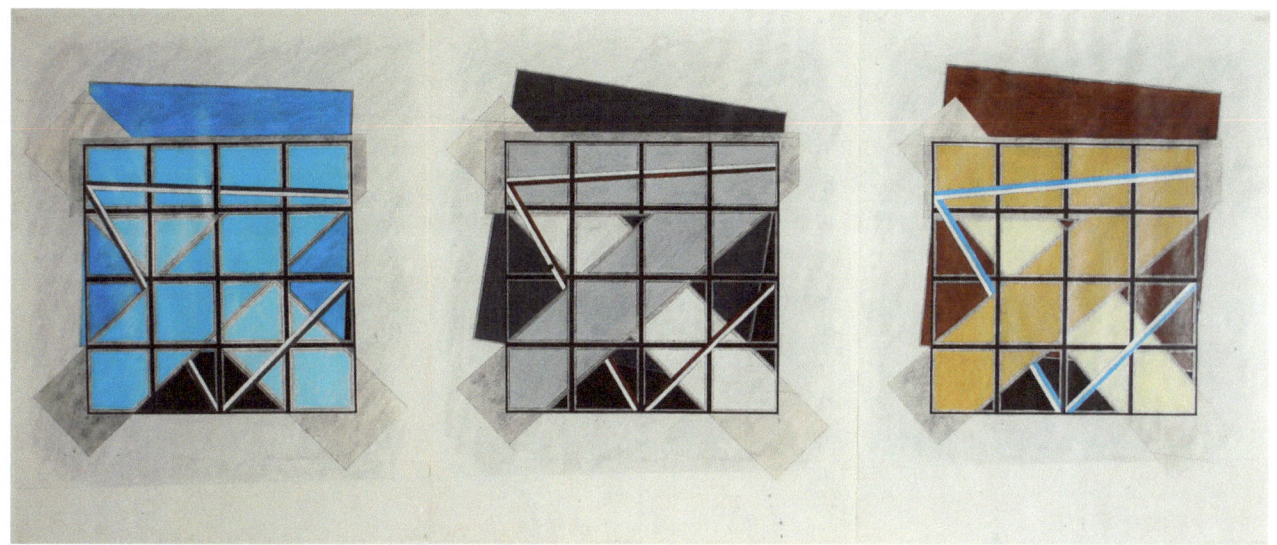

Adol, Beder, and Carnu, 1977
Acrylic on paper
23 x 57 inches
Cleveland Artists Foundation Collection

ends are perceived as being one continuous grouping that lies behind the darker rectangles.

Soon following, Mieczkowski began to move his paintings into a three-dimensional realm of constructions. His squares became individual compositions on masonite mounted to a "rack." Beyond these works, Mieczkowski began deconstruction of the square, shattering it into segments of cut out masonite that were then reconstructed with overlapping angles and forms as well as negative spaces that can become positive space. Works like *White China* from 1976 and the *Untitled (Construction)* from the 1980s show a forward movement in development.

White China remains relatively flat, with large segments of compact shapes cutting and overlapping others. Portions of the work also appear to be frame-like, suggesting that his composition also broke free from its confines as protrusions reach out from its edges. The grey scale palette of this piece makes a political statement when paired with its counterpart, *Red China*. Together the identical works, one in greys, the other in reds, are a commentary on the politics of a foreign nation which in the 1960s and 1970s were in a volatile state of political uncertainty.

Preparation to build these new constructions for Mieczkowski took the form of carefully planned drawings. The formative idea was completed in the sketching process and multiple drawings were made to explore different color combinations. *Adol, Beder, and Carnu* show the intricacies of thoughtful analysis of form. Slight variations in structure can be

13

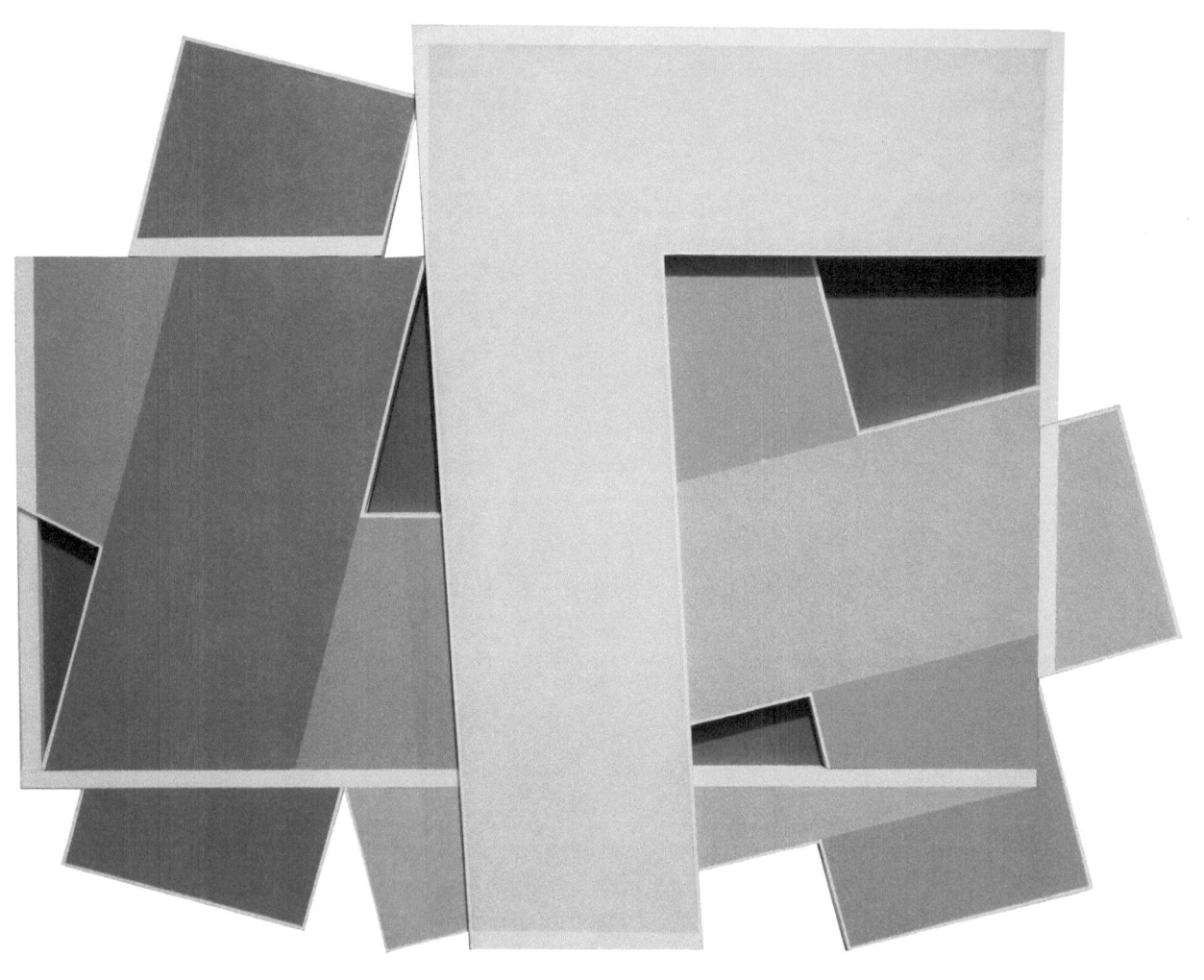

White China, 1976
Acrylic on masonite construction
36 x 46 inches
Collection of Constance Erdelac

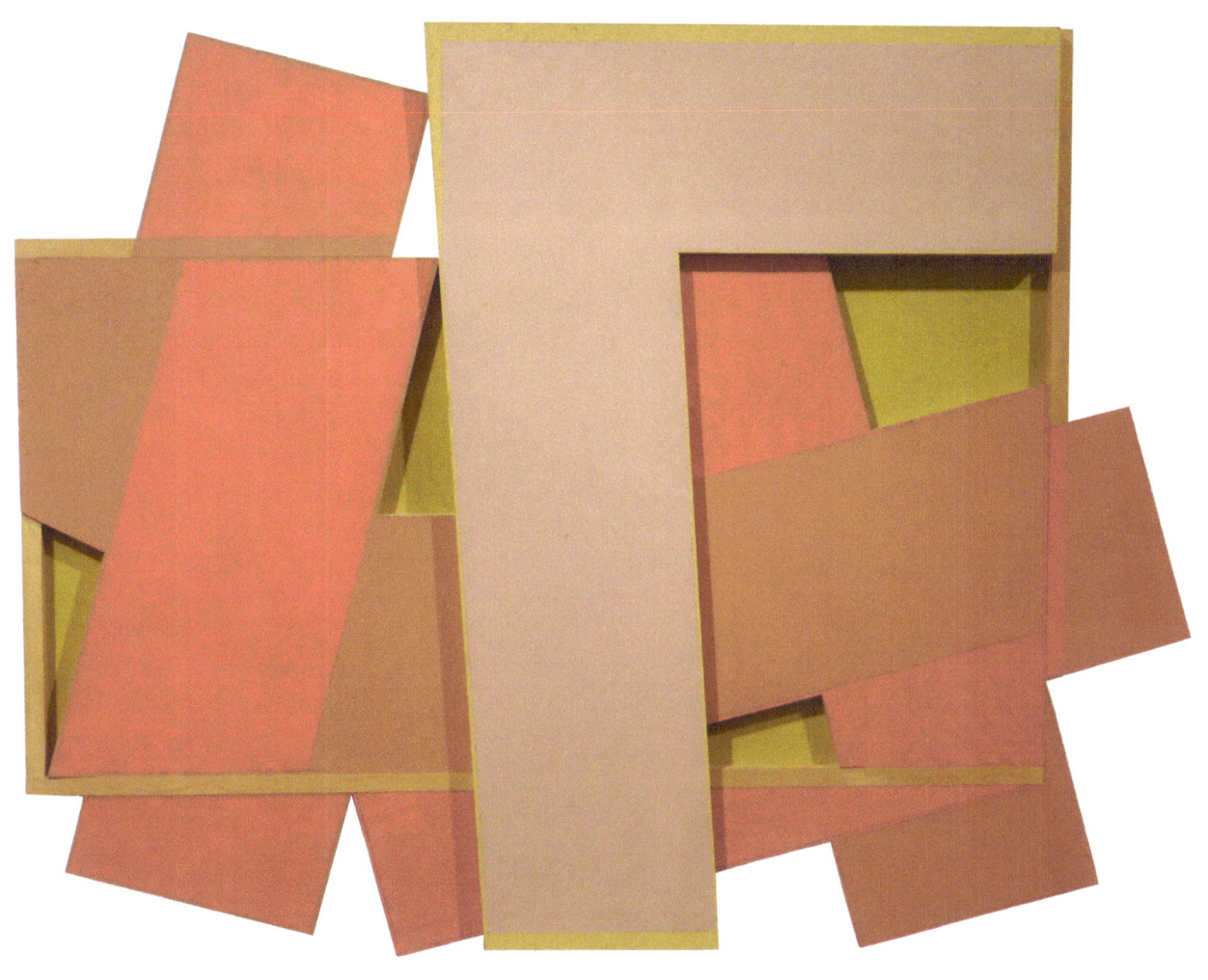

Red China, 1976
Acrylic on masonite construction
36 x 46 inches
Collection of Constance Erdelac

identified by close examination. Mieczkowski said of this process that the "formative reverie was cut to the minimum. It was as if there was no childhood for the idea."[8] All of the compositional problems were solved prior to the beginning of the construction process.

The constructions became even more elaborate and complex in the 1980s. By lifting the overlapping cut-out layers of either masonite or illustration board off of the pieces behind them, Mieczkowski began to explore the idea of parallax. Parallax is a property of perception that takes the different views from the eye to acquire a sense of depth. It also explains the displacement of an object in space in relationship to another when the viewer is in movement. The cut out shapes in Mieczkowski's constructions overlap the shapes behind and cover elements of the work depending on the viewers proximity and location. Adding to this effect is the painted geometric composition that is applied to the construction's surface. With the untitled construction, the white lines are painted on the piece as if it were a flat surface. When the viewer moves, the cut illustration board shifts and breaks up the white structure, creating a misalignment that alters depth perception.

Much in the same way, *Logic Loc* uses color to emphasize the contour of the main painted structure, while the cut and layered masonite creates another. While this piece is perceived to be one that focuses on the bright colors, the emphasis is on the white painted element of unbroken connected lines. The colors are in short segments that also assist in the fracturing of the picture plane according to the overlapping construction with the black areas acting to create a deeper space. This work shows how Mieczkowski made use of ideas from his black and white compositions in tandem with chromatic structures.

Mieczkowski emphasized the relationship of the constructions to the Constructivist movement by titling an exhibit of the work at the Great Northern Corporate Center Art Gallery "Neo-Constructivism" in 1987. Continually showing pride in Cleveland, he boldly stated

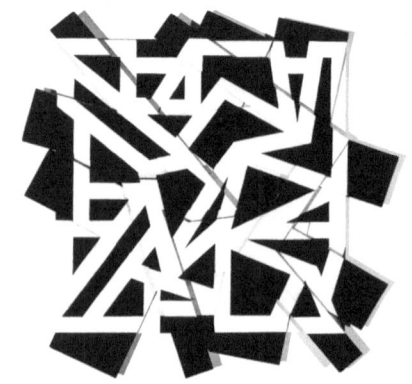

Untitled (Construction), 1980
18.5 x 17 inches
India ink on illustration board
Cleveland Artists Foundation Collection
Gift of Sharon and David Dean

16

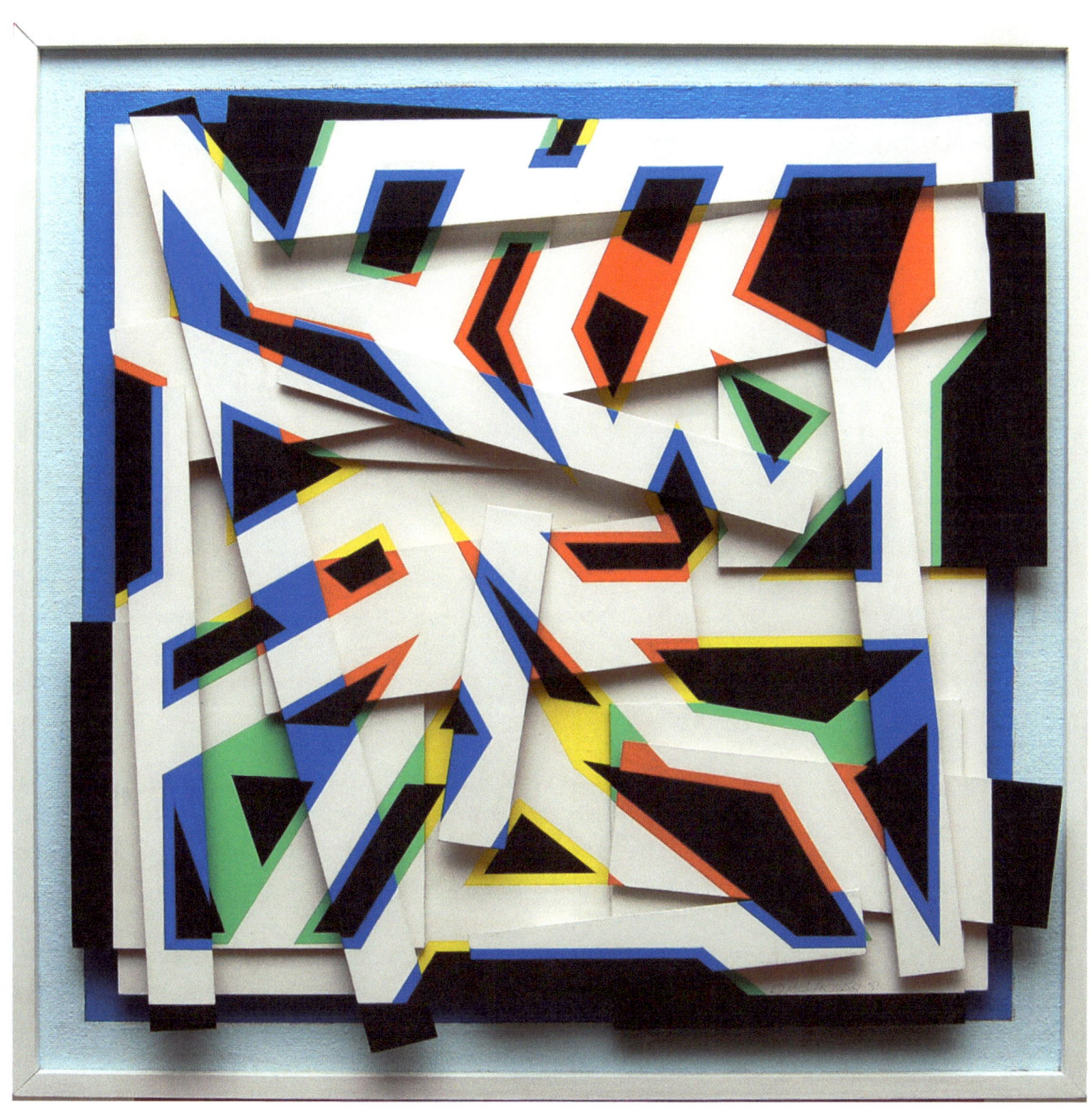

Logic Loc, 1982
Acrylic on wood construction
24 x 24 inches
Collection of Dave Tully

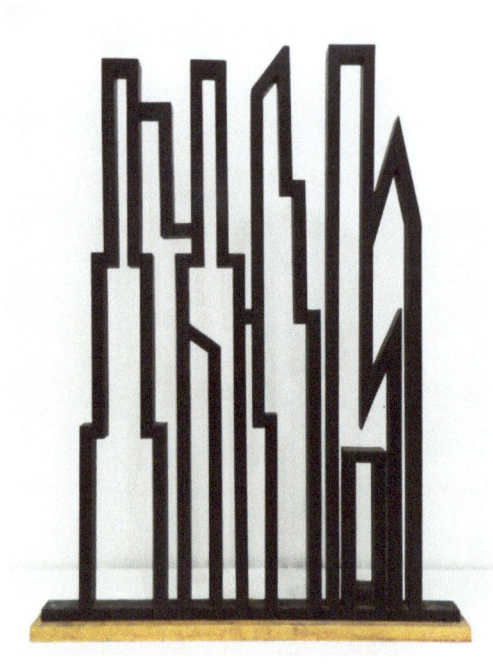

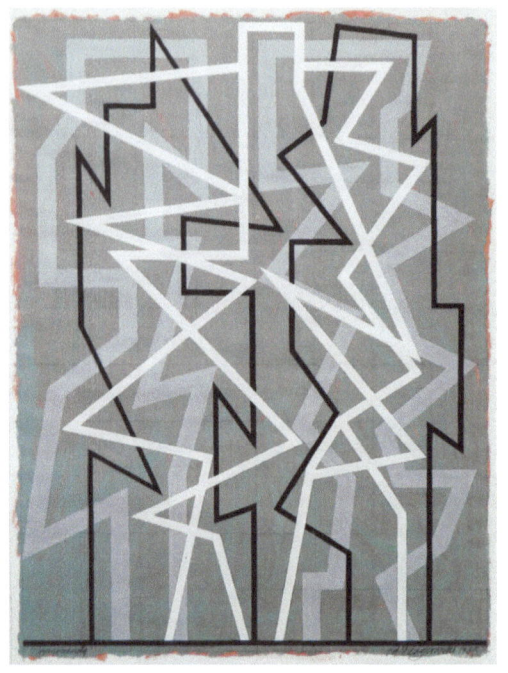

that "this is the new world head-quarters of Neo-Constructivism."[9] Mieczkowski also felt that Cleveland would one day become the center of the art world because of its geographic location between New York and Chicago.

Moving into freestanding sculpture, the *City series* pieces, like *Black Star City #1*, are painted solid black. Being representational of a city skyline, black brings together several connotations. First is of steel used in the construction of skyscrapers. These shapes are representations of buildings that became icons of the modern world, such as the black steel monolith masterpiece in New York, the Seagram building, by Ludwig Mies van der Rohe. Secondly, the title of the work and the color black allude to the darkness of night. As the wood construction draws the outline of the buildings, light is allowed to shine through, illuminating the interior much like the lights left on in offices after workers have left for the day. This interest in representational elements grew out of Mieczkowski's residing in two cities with the sculptures being what he calls "a dream city hybrid of Cleveland and New York."[10] The thickness of the linear structure, and its two-dimensionality directly

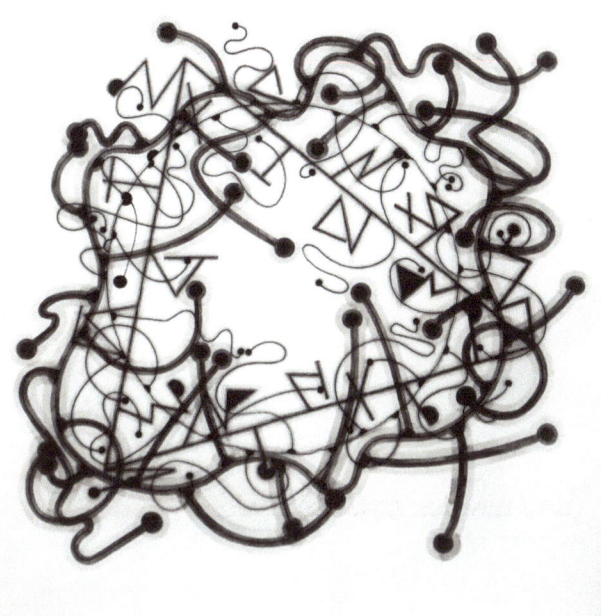

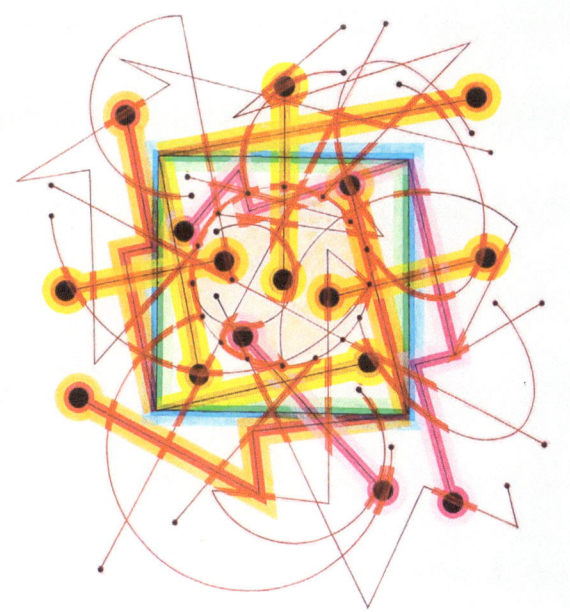

relate the *City series* pieces back to works on paper such as *Prominera*. This piece is also related to concerns of the city as it belongs to a body of work based on cranes and the industrial nature of urban construction. A black horizontal line near the bottom of the composition signifies the ground from which the bold white and black lines thrust upward in hectic diagonal movements of city growth. The subject of the city in both the sculptures and the work like *Prominera* elevate a typically non-referential style to one of social commentary, much in the same way Mieczkowski had done earlier with *White China* and *Red China*.

Becoming much looser in technique, Mieczkowski's paintings in the early 2000s combined his interests in different aspects of the sciences. *Galactica* and *Telomere Tumble #4* are interpretations of both star charts and human biology. While *Galactica's* black and white palette and title recall images of star charts, the curvilinear shapes also bring to mind dendrites found on neurons in the nervous system. *Telomere Tumble #4*, on the other hand, plainly suggests its subject as telomeres found on the end of a chromosome. Their function is to protect the chromosome from degradation during cell division. As a person ages, the shortening of telomeres

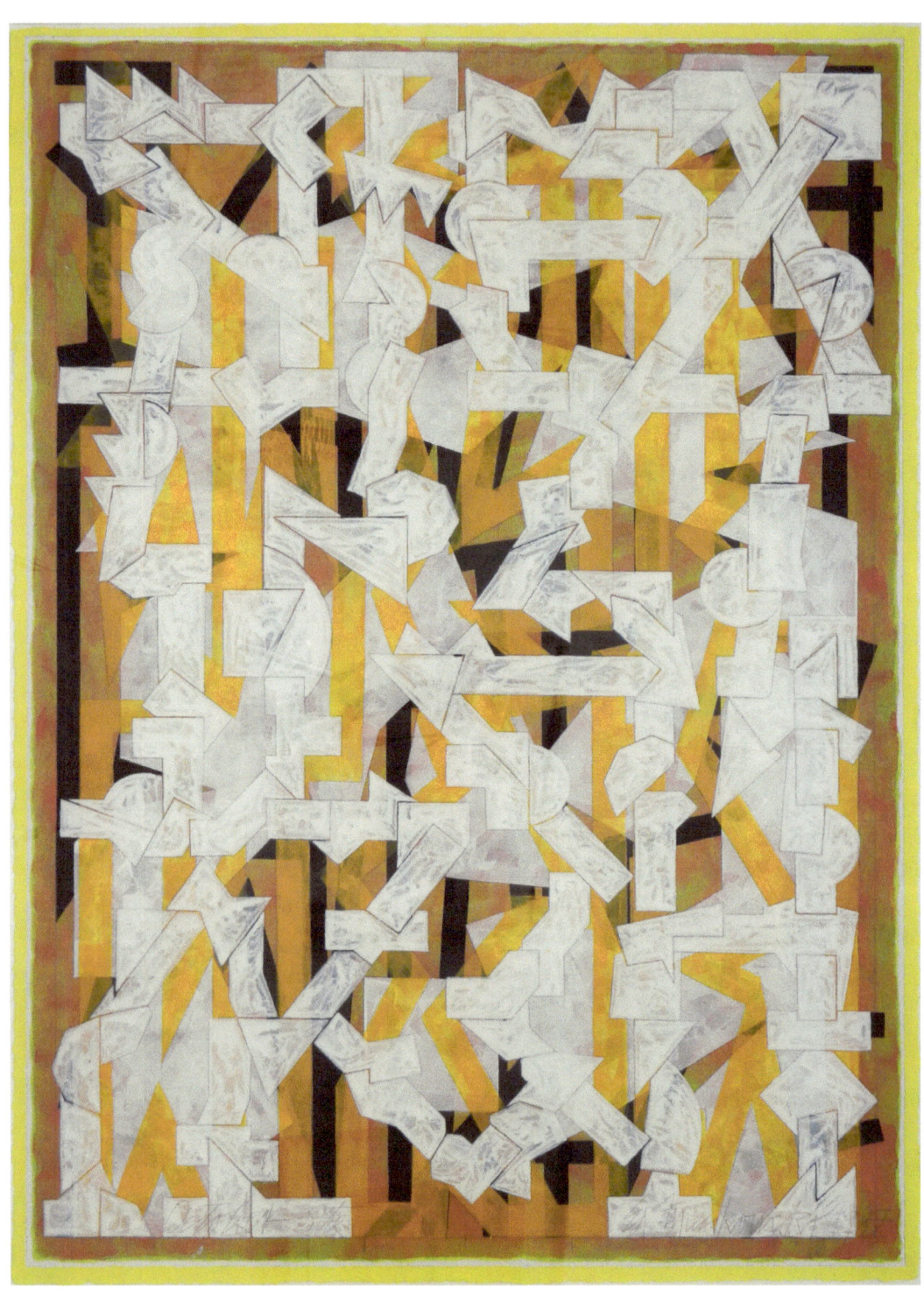

October Site, 1986
Acrylic on paper
45 x 32 inches
Progressive Art Collection

during division may not get replaced by the proper enzymes and could result in age-related diseases.[11] Visually similar, Mieczkowski abstracted charts and diagrams into a cohesive style composed of line and form that allowed the work to embrace the flatness of the painted surface.

Viewing the later works of Mieczkowski in black and white along with the earlier Anonima paintings it becomes evident that there is a progression of visual language even when the work appears to be completely unrelated. Segments can be visually dissected from a construction and similarities in form found in others. Relationships between the sculptures, constructions, drawings, and paintings emerge to heighten the viewers experience of the work. Through the use of black and white, Mieczkowski was able to explore perceptual cues in both studies and completed works, and then apply them to his experiments with color interactions. Valuable information can be gained by studying works in black and white, as the perceptual problems found within chromatic works are more easily grasped first in the achromatic palette. Examining Mieczkowski's black and white pieces with color counterparts shows his mastery of perceptual and informational art, a subject that is still filled with new discoveries.

END NOTES

1. Edwin Mieczkowski, "Remembering Frank," *Francis R. Hewitt* (Burlington: The Institute for Progressive Painting,1994), 12.

2. Benkert, Ernst, Francis Hewitt, and Edwin Mieczkowski, *Nova Tendencija 3* (Zagreb, Yugoslavia: Galerija Suvremene Umjetnosti, 1965), 7.

3. Rudolf Arnheim published his influential book Art and Visual Perception in 1954. Op artists in the 1960s explored ideas of gestalt – German for "form" – found in the text based on principles of Grouping, Figure/Ground, Contour and Closure.

4. Experimental psychology tested theories using scientific methods to research the mind and behavior, usually in a laboratory setting.

5. Ursula Korneitchouk, Geometric Abstraction: A Cleveland Tradition (Cleveland: The Cleveland Institute of Art, 1988), 10.

6. Michel Oren, "The Anonima Program for Perceptual Re-Education, 1960-70," Cleveland Studies in the History of Art, Vol. 5 (Cleveland: Cleveland Museum of Art, 2000), 61.

7. Ibid, 49.

8. Edwin Mieczkowski, Six Perspectives (Akron, Akron Art Museum, 1984), 24.

9. Helen Cullinan, "Artist shows new creative Level," Cleveland Plain Dealer, (March 2, 1987).

10. Hellen Cullinan, "Sculpture is his new Train of Thought," Cleveland Plain Dealer, (January 16, 1985), 26.

11. H. Jiang, Z. Ju, and K. L. Rudolp, "Telomere shortening and ageing," Z Gerontol Geriat 5, (2007) 314-315.

CHECKLIST*

Topopatop, 1965
Acrylic on masonite
24 x 24 inches
Private Collection

Ernst Benkert
Warsaw #1, 1964
Acrylic on masonite
24 x 24 inches
D. Wigmore Fine Art

Francis Hewitt
Munchin' Henries at Shaky Heights, 1965
Acrylic on masonite
24 x 24 inches
D. Wigmore Fine Art

Untitled, ISO-Metric series, 1965
Acrylic on masonite
44 x 41.5 inches
Cleveland Artists Foundation Collection

Study for ISO-Rung, 1965
Acrylic on masonite
30 x 30 inches
Rachel Davis Fine Arts

Small Bloc #2, 1966
Acrylic on masonite
24 x 24 inches
D. Wigmore Fine Art

Ice Rack, c. 1978
Acrylic on paper
22 x 30 inches
LewAllen Contemporary

White China, 1976
Acrylic on masonite construction
36 x 46 inches
Collection of Constance Erdelac

Untitled (Construction), 1980
18.5 x 17 inches
India ink on illustration board
Cleveland Artists Foundation Collection
Gift of Sharon and David Dean

Prominera, 1985
Acrylic on paper
40.5 x 30 inches
LewAllen Contemporary

Black Star City #1, c. 1980
Paint on wood sculpture
47 x 35 x 3 inches
Cleveland Artists Foundation Collection

Black Star #2, c. 1980
Paint on wood sculpture
45 x 39 x 3 inches
Cleveland Artists Foundation Collection

Untitled (City series), c. 1980
Paint on wood sculpture
44 x 38 x 3 inches
Cleveland Artists Foundation Collection

Throne, 1989
Acrylic on paper
41.5 x 32 inches
LewAllen Contemporary

Galactica, 2003
Acrylic on paper
44 x 41.5 inches
Tregoning and Co.

Adol, Beder, and Carnu, 1977
Acrylic on paper
23 x 57 inches
Cleveland Artists Foundation Collection

Telomere Tumble #4, c. 2000
Acrylic on paper
39 x 34 inches
Cleveland Artists Foundation Collection

Logic Loc, 1982
Acrylic on wood construction
24 x 24 inches
Collection of Dave Tully

October Site, 1986
Acrylic on paper
45 x 32 inches
Progressive Art Collection

Red China, 1976
Acrylic on masonite construction
36 x 46 inches
Collection of Constance Erdelac

Furnace II, 2007
Acrylic on canvas
36 x 36 inches
Tregoning and Co.

*All work is by Edwin Mieczkowski unless otherwise noted.

SELECTED SOLO & GROUP EXHIBITIONS

2012
"Ed Mieczkowski: Work from the 1960s"
(Solo) LewAllen Contemporary
Santa Fe, NM

2011
"Masters of Abstraction"
The Reinberger Galleries
Cleveland Institute of Art
Cleveland, OH

"CLE OP: Cleveland Op Art Pioneers"
Cleveland Museum of Art
Cleveland, OH

2010
"Op Out of Ohio"
D. Wigmore Fine Art
New York, NY

2007
"Optic Nerve"
Columbus Museum of Art
Columbus, OH

"Optic Verve" (Solo)
Tregoning & Co.
Cleveland, OH

2006
"Visual Paradox" (Solo)
LewAllen Contemporary
Santa Fe, NM

2001
"Harmonic Forms on the Edge:
Geometric Abstraction in Cleveland"
Cleveland Artists Foundation
Cleveland, OH

1987
"Neo-Constructivism" (Solo)
Great Northern Corporate Center
North Olmsted, OH

1984
"Six Perspectives"
Akron Art Museum
Akron, OH

1981
"Some New Works" (Solo)
The New Gallery of Contemporary Art
Cleveland, OH

1979
"Visual Logic"
Cleveland Institute of Art
Cleveland, OH

1972
"Grids"
Institute of Contemporary Art
University of Pennsylvania
Philadelphia, PH

1969
"The Square in Painting"
The American Federation of the Arts
New York, NY

1966
"Black White and Gray Paintings"
Anonima Group Gallery
New York, NY

1965
"The Responsive Eye"
Mueseum of Modern Art
New York, NY

"New Tendency 3"
Galerija Suvremene Umjetnosti
Zagreb, Yugoslavia

1964
"Movement 2"
Galerie Denise Rene,
Paris, France

"Vibrations Eleven"
Martha Jackson Gallery
New York, NY